Queen of Inventions

How the Sewing Machine Changed the World

Laurie Carlson

The Millbrook Press   Brookfield, Connecticut

Published by The Millbrook Press, Inc.
2 Old New Milford Road
Brookfield, Connecticut 06804
www.millbrookpress.com

Carlson, Laurie M., 1952-
Queen of inventions:how the sewing machine changed the world/by Laurie Carlson.
p. cm.
Summary: Looks at the history of sewing and how it was transformed in the 1850s
when an American inventor, Isaac Singer, not only invented a practical sewing
machine, but also a way for everyone to afford one.
ISBN 0-7613-2706-1 (lib. bdg.)
1. Sewing machines—History—Juvenile literature.   2. Singer, Isaac Merritt,
1811-1875—Juvenile literature.   [1. Sewing machines.   2. Singer, Isaac Merritt,
1811-1875.   3. Inventions.]   I. Title.
TJ1507 .C37 2003   681'.7677—dc21   2002001584

Photographs courtesy of North Wind Picture Archives: pp. 1, 3 (right), 4 (right), 5
(right), 6, 7 (left), 10 (left), 11 (left), 18 (left), 23, 25; Corbis: pp. 3 (left ©
Christie's Images), 4 (left), 7 (right © Archivo Iconografico, S.A.), 24 (right © Lake
County Museum), 26, 27 (© Underwood & Underwood), 30 (© Lake County
Museum); Underwood Photo Archives, Inc.: pp. 5 (left), 18 (right), 20, 21 (top left;
bottom left), 22, 29 (top); Smithsonian Institution: pp. 8 (both), 9 (all), 10 (right),
11 (right), 12 (all), 14, 23, 24 (middle); Nebraska State Historical Society: p. 15
(#RG2608-1468); Library of Congress: pp. 17 (left), 19, 21 (top right; bottom right),
24 (left); State Historical Society of Wisconsin Visual Materials Archive: pp. 16
(top: Whi-3735/Singer Collection; left:Whi-3736/Singer Collection; right: New York
Public Library-3733), 17 (right: Whi-3732), 28 (Whi-3734), 29 (bottom: Whi-3729).

Long ago, people sat all day and sometimes into the night stitching with needle and thread.

That was the only way to make ships' sails for going across the sea, wagon covers for traveling west,

3

flags to fly in glory,

wedding dresses for the big day,

Girls spent hours every day learning how to make tiny, careful stitches that would be strong. They needed to know how to stitch

baby clothing for the little ones, and everything anyone wore.

well because when they grew up they would need to make all the clothes their family wore. They also had to stitch towels, and blankets, and bedsheets, and tablecloths, and curtains. It was a lot of stitching, and a lot of hard work.

Not everyone was good at stitching. Sometimes things didn't turn out quite right.

No matter—stitching was so much work that people wore their clothing for years, sometimes turning it inside out to make it last longer.

Wealthy families hired tailors to sew suits, or paid girls called seamstresses to come to their homes to sew dresses and shirts. It took lots of time to try on the garments as they were being made. It took lots of work to make them. Even wealthy people didn't have a lot of clothes.

A man in France,

Barthélemy Thimonniér,

thought that a machine that stitched would be useful, so he built some simple machines to sew uniforms for the French army. But in 1841 an angry mob of tailors tore down the doors of his workshop and threw all the machines out the windows because they were afraid the machines would drive them out of business.

Isaac Singer

In America, several people tried making stitching machines, but none worked very well or very fast. Isaac Singer was one of these inventors. He had spent years trying to earn a living for his family as an actor, but had failed at that. He had invented a clever tool to drill rock and a machine to carve wooden letters, but he didn't make much money.

It was 1850. Isaac was sitting in a rented workshop in Boston, Massachusetts, ready to give up on the letter machine, when a friend suggested he try making a sewing machine. Isaac realized that if any machine could make a fellow rich, a machine that stitched seams could do it!

Isaac worked for eleven days and nights building a sewing machine that could be powered by a foot pedal called a treadle. But when he tried stitching, the thread bunched up in loops. This machine was a failure, just like the others.

Elias Howe created a chain-stitch sewing machine in 1844, but it sewed poorly and no one was interested in buying it. He went back to farming. Years later, Singer and other sewing machine manufacturers paid Howe for his patent and he ended up a multi-millionaire.

Elias Howe

That night an idea came to him. A spring could be used to pull the thread tightly so it wouldn't curl up. His son found a spring from a toy popgun, and Isaac hurried back to the workshop with it. The spring worked! The machine sewed stitches that were tight and smooth.

Isaac now had a chance at success. His family had been living on ten dollars a week. If he sold sewing machines, his family would have a home of their own and everything they wanted. Isaac Singer found a business partner, and they placed a newspaper ad for **SEWING BY MACHINERY**.

Crowds gathered to watch contests between the sewing machine and the fastest hand stitchers. A machine could sew nearly one thousand stitches a minute! Even the fastest tailor or seamstress couldn't match that. People were so impressed that one magazine even called the new machine

"The Queen of Inventions."

Of course, everyone wanted to own a sewing machine. Isaac Singer set up a small workshop to make more of the machines. Every tiny part had to be made by hand and fitted together. The machines were very expensive. Few people had enough money to buy one.

Isaac realized that his sewing machine idea would never make him rich unless everyone could afford to buy one. He tried to make the machines cheaper to build by making every part exactly alike, so the machines could be put together quickly. That helped, but still the machines were costly. For a while, sales were slow. Singer thought he might have to go out of business. He *had* to figure out a way to get more people to buy his machines. He decided to take a risk. He would let people pay five dollars, take the machine home with them, and send him the rest of the money a little at a time.

It worked! People saved money for a down payment, sent the money to Singer, and he shipped them a machine. The people paid the rest of the money by installments, a little every month, until their machines were paid for. The best part was, they could use the machine to earn money to make the payments.

People needed to learn how to use the new invention, so salespeople went to customers' homes to show them how to operate the clever machines. Sewing-machine sales agents traveled all over the country on trains and coaches. They taught Chinese ladies how to use their new machines in San Francisco, and showed ranch families how to adjust, oil, and stitch with their machines on the Dakota prairie. They taught customers in tiny fishing villages, in gold-mining camps, and in New York City.

Sewing machines spread to many countries around the world.

One machine could earn the owner more than five dollars a day. With a machine, mothers could sew at home for pay while their children slept.

Men could tote their machines on their backs every day to clothing factories, where they could earn more money than tailors could ever make sewing by hand.

Ladies could have lots of ruffles, flounces, and frills on their dresses. Skirts got fuller and fuller until they took up almost the whole room!

Sewing machines are useful for much more than making clothing. In 1911 a scientific expedition set out to explore Antarctica, and took a sewing machine along. It was used to repair the leather harnesses used by the sled dogs. During World War II, workers in factories full of sewing machines turned out parachutes for airmen from large pieces of silk. Today, at the Rocky Mountain firefighting center in Montana, smoke jumpers sew their own parachutes to use when they are airlifted to fight forest fires.

Sewing with machines made a real difference because everything could be made much more quickly. Once it had taken a hand stitcher fifteen minutes to sew a man's hat. With a machine, it could be done in one minute. One person could sew as many boys' caps by machine as ten people could by hand in the same length of time. It had taken a tailor six days of steady hand-stitching to make one overcoat. With a machine, it took only three days.

Everything that had been made by hand could now be stitched speedily and sturdily with a machine. Machines were used to stitch boots and shoes, as well as suitcases, horse collars, mailbags, grain sacks, corsets, purses, caps, leather gloves, parasols, straw hats, theater curtains, military uniforms, flags, fire hoses, and even hot-air balloons.

By 1870, factories filled with hundreds of sewing machines were turning out thousands of garments. One town had over three thousand machines, all making shirts. Stores sprang up where customers could try on garments before they bought them. Mail-order catalogs made it easy for people to buy clothing from anywhere in the country.

RULES FOR MEASUREMENT.

Anyone with an ordinary tape measure and a little care can take a correct measurement that will insure a good fit. Do not draw the measure too tight.

CHILD'S SUIT.

MEASUREMENTS FOR CHILD'S SUIT.

		INCHES.
For Length of,	E to F,	....
" Sleeve, Arm Bent,	A to B to C to D,	....
" Breast, around body under Coat,	L to M,	....
" Waist, around body under the Coat,	G to H,	....
" Outside Seam of Pants,	H to I,	....
" Inside " "	J to K,	....

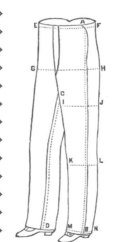

LONG PANTS.

MEASUREMENTS FOR LONG PANTS.

		INCHES.
For Outside Seam,	A to B,	....
" Inside " .	C to D,	....
" Waist, around body,	E to F,	....
" Seat	G to H,	....
" Thigh,	I to J,	....
" Knee,	K to L,	....
' Bottom,	M to N,	....

1   2

23

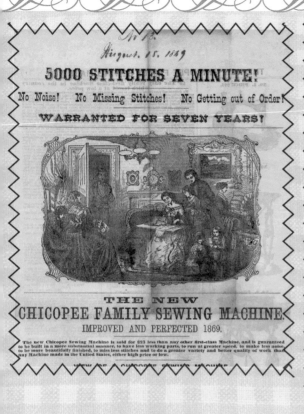

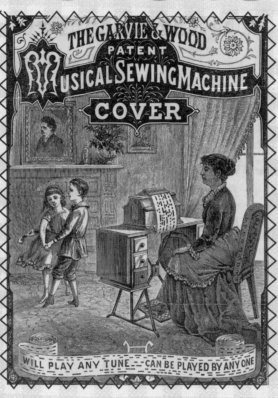

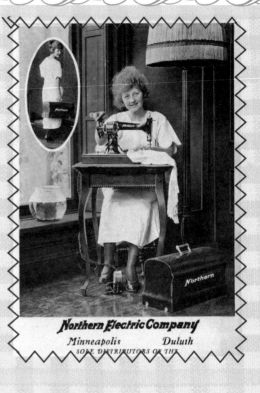

Many people besides Isaac Singer went into business manufacturing sewing machines in the 1870s. At one time there were more than two hundred companies making sewing machines. Inventors kept trying to improve how sewing machines worked. In the years after Singer introduced his machine, inventors filed 3,500 patents for ideas to improve sewing machines. Singer bought many of their ideas to include in his own machines.

As times changed, horses and wagons were replaced by delivery vans and motorcycle sidecars, which were just right for delivering sewing machines to customers' homes. Soon sewing machines powered by electricity worked even faster than the ones with foot treadles. People could buy improved machines by trading in their old one as the down payment.

Machines gave freedom to people who could afford to buy clothing already made up, and opportunity to many who used sewing machines to earn a living. Women could use their machine to make money at home, or they could find jobs in factories, where rows of sewing machines whirred into the night. With sewing no longer taking up all their days, more girls had time for school.

Isaac Singer's sewing machine factory kept growing until it covered 72 acres in New Jersey and had 9,000 workers. The Singer Company sent agents all over the world to sell machines. Singer factories sprang up in Canada, Scotland, Germany, Austria, and

Russia. Isaac moved his family to France, then to England, to keep an eye on his factories. By selling machines around the world, Isaac Singer's company became the most successful sewing-machine maker in history. Singer's family, which had once lived on ten dollars a week, enjoyed a mansion with a grand piano, six carriages, and ten horses, and all the food they desired.

Isaac Singer? Well, he had a stage built in his mansion so he could go back to his first dream—acting!

Excerpt from "The Song of the Shirt"

With fingers weary and worn,

With eyelids heavy and red,

A woman sat, in unwomanly rags,

Plying her needle and thread—

Stitch! stitch! stitch!

In poverty, hunger, and dirt

And still with a voice of dolorous pitch—

Would that its tone could reach the rich!—

She sang this "Song of the Shirt!"

(A popular ditty of the early 1800s
written by Thomas Hood that tells
of the hardships of women hand-stitchers
before the advent of the sewing machine)

For Further Reading

100 Inventions That Shaped World History, by Bill Yenne. Bluewood Books, 1993.

Good Girl Work: Factories, Sweatshops, and How Women Changed Their Role in the American Workforce, by Catherine Gourley. Millbrook Press, 1999.

Inventors and Inventions, by Lorraine Hopping Egan. Scholastic, 1999.

The Kids' Invention Book, by Arlene Erlbach. Lerner Publications, 1999.

My First Machine Sewing Book, by Winky Cherry. Palmer Pletsch Publishing, 1995.

The Sewing Machine, by Beatrice Siegel. Walker & Company, 1984.

Women Invent: Two Centuries of Discoveries That Have Shaped Our World, by Susan Casey. Chicago Review Press, 1997.

On the Internet

FamilyFun Activities & Crafts: Sewing & Fabric
www.family.go.com/crafts/sew/
Home Sewing Association Kids Korner
www.sewing.org/html/kids.html
Singer: Corporate History
www.singerco.com

Bibliography

Brandon, Ruth. *Singer and the Sewing Machine: A Capitalist Romance*. Philadelphia: J.B. Lippincott Company, 1977.

Cooper, Grace Rogers. *The Sewing Machine: Its Invention and Development*. Washington, D.C.: National Museum of History and Technology, Smithsonian Institution, 1976.

Derry, T. K. and Trevor I. Williams. *A Short History of Technology: From the Earliest Times to A.D. 1900*. New York: Dover Publications, Inc., 1993.

Lewton, Frederick Lewis. *The Servant in the House: A Brief History of the Sewing Machine*. Smithsonian Publication 3056. Washington, D.C.: Government Printing Office, 1930.

Scott, John. *Genius Rewarded, or the Story of the Sewing Machine*. New York: J. J. Caulon, 1880.